How we USE materials

Paper

Holly Wallace

W

First published in 2006 by
Franklin Watts
338 Euston Road
London NW1 3BH

Franklin Watts Australia
Hachette Children's Books
Level 17/207 Kent Street
Sydney NSW 2000

ISBN-10: 0 7496 6458 4
ISBN-13: 978 0 7496 6458 9
Dewey classification: 676

Art director: Jonathan Hair
Series designed and created for Franklin Watts by Painted Fish Ltd.
Designer: Rita Storey
Editor: Fiona Corbridge

Picture credits
Corbis Sygma/Annebicque Bernard p. 9 (top), Corbis/Ariel Skelley p. 16, p. 27
(bottom); istockphoto.com p. 8, p. 9 (bottom), p. 13, p. 15, p. 17 (bottom), p. 18,
p. 19 (top), p. 21, p. 25, p. 26, p. 27 (top); Tudor Photography p. 3, p. 5, pp. 6–7,
pp. 10–11, p. 12, p. 14, p. 17 (top), p. 19 (bottom), p. 20, p. 22, p. 23, p. 24.

Cover images: Tudor Photography, Banbury

A CIP catalogue record for this book is available from the British Library.

Printed in China

Contents

Words in **bold** are in the glossary.

What is paper?

Paper is a **material**. We can use it to make lots of different things.

- Cards, envelopes, books and newspapers are all made from paper.

Paper objects, like these bags and wrapping paper, can be **printed** with different colours and patterns.

Tissues are made from soft, thin paper, which can soak up, or **absorb**, liquids well.

Paper cups and plates can be used once and thrown away.

Paper keywords
Soft
Printed
Material
Absorb

Where does paper come from?

We make paper from tiny **fibres** that come from the wood of trees.

The wood is cut into logs and taken to a factory called a **papermill**.

Here the wood is chopped into tiny pieces called chips. The chips are mixed with water and **chemicals**. Then machines mash them into a thick paste called **pulp**.

The pulp is spread out in a thin layer on a machine and dried to make paper. The finished paper is put on big rolls or cut into sheets.

Paper keywords

Fibres
Papermill
Pulp

What is paper like?

We use paper in many ways. Different kinds of paper are useful for different jobs.

Paper can be made into thin, smooth sheets, which are good for writing on. Paper can also be bent and folded to make envelopes for letters.

Coloured paper is made by adding chemicals called **dyes** to the paper pulp.

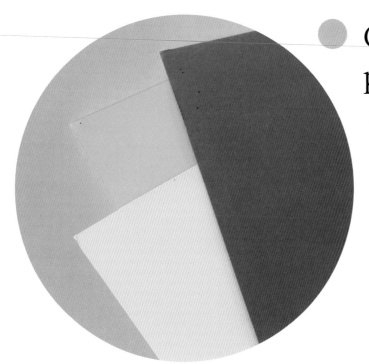

Card is thick, stiff paper. It can be made in many different colours.

Cardboard is made from layers of card and paper. Cardboard is stronger than ordinary paper and does not tear so easily. We use cardboard to make boxes because it is thick and strong.

Paper keywords

Dyes
Cardboard
Card

Paper for writing and painting

Paper is a good material for writing and painting on. Ink and paint stick to paper well.

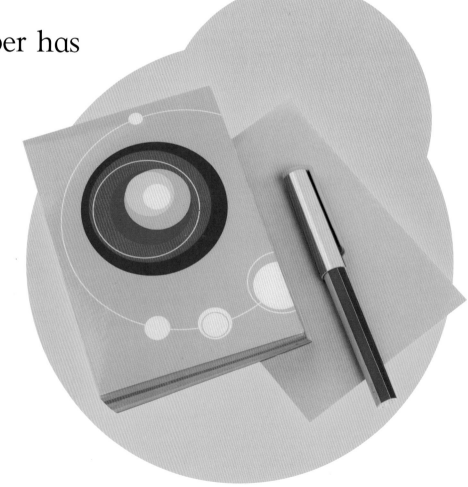

Writing paper has a special smooth **coating**. The ink sticks to the coating and does not soak into the paper.

If you write on paper with a pencil, you can use an eraser to rub out any mistakes.

Some artists use watery paints called watercolours. They paint on special thick paper, which absorbs the paint.

Paper keywords

Coating
Smooth

Paper for printing

Most paper is used for printing books, newspapers and magazines.

● The pages inside a book are printed on book paper. This kind of paper is thin and white. The book's cover is made of cardboard. It **protects** the pages and holds them together.

The paper goes through a machine called a **printing press**. The press prints words and pictures on the paper.

Banknotes are printed on paper that has strong fibres in it. This makes the paper difficult to tear, so the banknotes last longer.

Paper keywords

Printing
Printing press
Banknotes

Wrapping paper

We use some kinds of paper for wrapping up presents or to send parcels by post.

Paper is good for wrapping things because it is easy to cut and fold. We can use tape or glue to stick pieces of paper together.

Wrapping paper comes in many different colours. Some paper has patterns and pictures printed on it.

Mr J Green
12 Park Terrace
Brampton
DD2 4PU

Miss S Percy
23 Silver Street
Trentan
TW2 9TY

Brown paper has fibres from cotton plants added to it. This makes it stronger. Brown paper is good for wrapping parcels that will be sent through the post.

Paper keywords

Wrapping
Colours

Paper packaging

Factories use paper and card to hold and protect the things they make. This is called **packaging**.

● Strong cardboard boxes are used to hold heavy things, such as computers and televisions. The cardboard helps to stop the things inside getting broken.

Some boxes are made from pulp that has been made shaped in a **mould**. Eggboxes are a special shape to stop the eggs moving about.

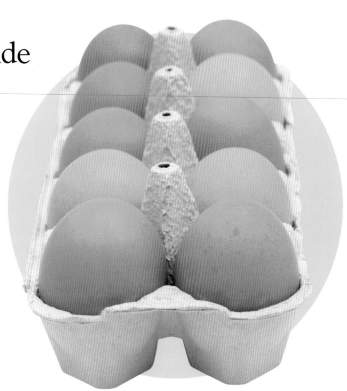

We buy milk and fruit juice in card **cartons**. Card is not **waterproof** so it has to be coated with **wax** to stop the liquid soaking through it.

Orange Juice

Paper keywords
Cartons
Waterproof
Packaging

Paper decorations

All kinds of decorations can be made from coloured and patterned paper.

- We can make **paperchains** to decorate a room for a party. It is fun to throw **paper streamers** like these.

- Party plates and cups are made from card. They are **disposable**, so we throw them away after use.

These model ducks are made from **papier mâché**. It is made from wet paper and glue. It goes hard when it dries.

We can fold paper into all kinds of shapes, such as this animal. Folding paper into shapes in this way is called **origami**.

Paper keywords

Disposable
Papier mâché
Origami

Paper in the home

Paper is good for decorating our homes. It is also very useful in the kitchen.

● Walls can be covered with **wallpaper** instead of paint. Wallpaper is thick and heavy paper, which comes in rolls. It is printed with different patterns and colours. It has to be glued on to a wall.

Paper towels, paper napkins, tissues and toilet paper are made from paper that is good at soaking up liquids.

Sandpaper is made by gluing sand on to tough paper to give it a rough surface. We use sandpaper to make wood smooth and rub away old paint.

Paper keywords

Wallpaper
Sandpaper

Paper at school

Look around your classroom.
You use lots of paper objects
at school.

- You write in paper exercise books.
Teachers make lists and posters
out of paper and card
and put them on
the wall.

To print out words or pictures from a computer, you need a printer filled with sheets of paper.

Is your classroom decorated with paintings and collages? A collage is a picture made from glued paper shapes.

Recycling paper

We throw away millions of tonnes of paper every day. But a lot of this should be **recycled**.

Old paper is collected for recycling. It is mashed up to make a pulp. This is mixed with new pulp and made into new paper.

Most recycled paper is used to make cardboard and newspapers. Some is used to make tissues, paper towels and toilet paper.

We can also reuse paper. One way of using old newspaper again is to tear it into strips and use it to make cosy bedding for a pet.

Paper keywords

Recycled
Mashed
Tear

Glossary

Absorb Soak up liquids.

Banknotes Pieces of paper which are worth a certain amount of money.

Brown paper Thick, strong paper made with cotton fibres. It is used for wrapping parcels.

Cardboard A type of thin board made from layers of card and paper.

Cartons Boxes made from light card, which are used for holding milk, fruit juice and other types of food and drink.

Chemicals Special substances used to do many jobs, including making wood softer to make paper.

Coating An outer layer.

Disposable Designed to be thrown away after use.

Dyes Substances used to colour paper.

Fibres Very thin threads. The fibres in paper come from trees and plants.

Material Something out of which other objects can be made.

Mould A shape that pulp is poured into to make the same shape.

Origami A special way of folding paper to make it into objects and decorations. It comes from Japan.

Packaging Boxes, cartons and envelopes in which other objects are packed. Factories also use paper and card packaging to protect the things they make when they are sold in shops.

Paperchains Decorations made from a chain of paper loops.

Papermill A factory where paper is made.

Paper streamers Long, thin pieces of paper used as decorations.

Papier mâché A material made from wet paper and glue, which goes hard when it dries.

Printed Marked with words or pictures.

Printing press A machine that marks paper with words or pictures.

Protects Stops something getting dirty or spoiled.

Pulp A mixture of wood chips, water and chemicals, which has been mashed together.

Recycled 'Recycling' means to collect used materials so that they can be specially treated and used again.

Wallpaper Large sheets of coloured or patterned paper pasted on to walls to decorate them.

Waterproof Does not let water pass through.

Wax A smooth, oily material that does not let liquid through it.

Index